Wild Rides

Wild About

Monster Trucks

J. Poolos

PowerKiDS press

New York

For Helena

Published in 2008 by The Rosen Publishing Group, Inc.
29 East 21st Street, New York, NY 10010

First Edition

Editor: Amelie von Zumbusch
Book Design: Greg Tucker
Photo Researcher: Nicole Pristash

Photo Credits: Cover, pp. 5, 11, 13, 19 © Getty Images; pp. 7, 9 © Shutterstock.com; p. 15, 17, 21 by Eric Stern.

Library of Congress Cataloging-in-Publication Data

Poolos, Jamie.
  Wild about monster trucks / J. Poolos.
     p. cm. — (Wild rides)
  Includes index.
  ISBN-13: 978-1-4042-3791-9 (library binding)
  ISBN-10: 1-4042-3791-7 (library binding)
  1. Monster trucks—Juvenile literature. I. Title.
  TL230.15.P659 2008
  629.224—dc22

                                        2006101983

Manufactured in the United States of America

Contents

Monster-Truck Madness

A monster truck is a pickup truck that has giant wheels and tires. Monster trucks appear at shows, where they **perform** for crowds. Monster trucks can be driven up and over large objects. These trucks can even be driven up on top of cars to crush, or flatten, them. Monster trucks also fly over jumps. At some shows, two monster trucks race across a course, or path, with cars to crush and jumps.

Crowds love monster trucks! These trucks are loud and powerful. Crowds cheer on the drivers when they crush things and roll the trucks over.

The monster truck Rocket is shown crushing cars at a monster-truck rally, or show, in Anaheim, California.

Big Wheeling

Although monster trucks are shaped like pickup trucks, monster trucks are **custom** made. Monster-truck builders start by building a strong frame out of steel tubes, or pipes. The builders put large **engines** that make 2,000 **horsepower** into their trucks. They add supersized **shock absorbers**.

Then the builders add giant wheels and tires with huge treads, or lines, in them. Monster-truck tires are taller than most people! One cool thing about monster trucks is that drivers can steer, or direct, all four wheels separately. Drivers use controls called gears to make the wheels turn.

The big treads in monster-truck wheels help keep the trucks from slipping, or sliding.

Cool Paint Jobs

Monster trucks are a bit like cartoon characters. Both monster trucks and cartoon characters are colorful. Both have interesting names. Bigfoot and **Grave** Digger are the names of two well-liked monster trucks. These trucks have paint jobs that look like the paint on race cars. Monster trucks often have pictures of animals, like bears. Some trucks have flames on them.

One monster truck, the **Predator**, has a front shaped like the face of a black panther. Black panthers are powerful cats. The Predator has eyes and a mouth full of teeth painted on it.

This monster truck has a picture of early people hunting an animal called a woolly mammoth on it.

Behind the Wheel

Since monster trucks are so big and powerful, they are hard to drive. Monster-truck drivers sit in the middle of the truck. A **harness** holds the driver in the seat when the monster truck jumps over cars or rolls over. The driver uses a steering wheel to turn the front wheels. Drivers use a control called a switch to turn the back wheels.

When a truck crashes, the driver must use a switch called a kill switch to turn off the engine. Monster trucks have three kill switches. The driver turns off the engine with the nearest kill switch.

Along with harnesses, monster-truck drivers wear hard hats called helmets to keep themselves safe.

The First Monster Trucks

In the 1970s, truck racer Bob Chandler wanted to show people how well his custom truck parts worked. Chandler made a video of Bigfoot, his truck with giant wheels, driving over cars. A **promoter** saw the video, and soon Chandler was crushing cars in front of large crowds.

In 1985, promoters began holding special monster-truck events. As the sport grew, more and more people came to watch the big trucks race, jump, and crash. In 1988, the Monster Truck Racing Association was formed to create rules for a **championship**. Today, monster-truck events are held all over the country.

Bigfoot is seen here crushing cars at a monster-truck show in Anaheim, California, in 1989.

Monster-Truck Teams

Each truck has a team backing it. The team is made up of the owner, the driver, and **mechanics**. Sometimes, teams are run by families and the owner is the driver. Teams travel the country with big trailers. Trailers are big, wheeled objects that hold the monster truck, extra truck parts, and tools.

The extra parts and tools come in handy. Because so much force is put on the trucks, they break down easily. The **axles** bend or break, and shock absorbers are destroyed. It takes lots of work just to keep a monster truck running for one weekend.

Mike Hawkins is the owner and driver of the monster truck Equalizer, seen behind him.

Drag Racing

Monster-truck shows are fun to watch. The main event at a monster-truck show is called drag racing. In a drag race, monster trucks race over a course filled with things to jump over. Some courses have cars that the trucks are driven up over and crush. Other courses have dirt jumps or sticky mud, called mud bogs.

The trucks line up at the starting line. Someone drops a flag, and the trucks tear off down the course and over the jumps. Sometimes the trucks pop huge **wheelies** or flip over. The first truck to cross the finish line wins!

Monster trucks Raminator and Rammunition are shown here racing against each other at this August 2006 show.

Freestyle

Monster-truck shows also have freestyle events. Freestyle events first appeared in the early 1990s. Some of the drivers whose trucks had been beaten in drag races wanted to find other ways to show off for the crowd. They asked the event's promoters if they could perform between races. Freestyle was born!

In a freestyle event, trucks go all over the course, jumping, crushing cars, and **spinning doughnuts**. The crowds love when the drivers push the trucks so far that they break or crash. Freestyle is now as well liked as racing. There is even a freestyle championship.

Crowds clap and shout as monster trucks crush cars at freestyle events.

Bear Foot

Bear Foot is one of the best-known monster trucks. It was made in 1979 by Fred Shafer. Bear Foot was the second monster truck ever. The truck is named for Shafer's two pet American black bears. The front of the truck looks like a bear's face. The bear has sharp claws and big, strong teeth.

Bear Foot looks cool, and it can perform, too. In 1993, Bear Foot became the first truck to win three World Monster Truck Championships. In 1996, it was listed in the *Guinness Book of World Records* for the world's longest outdoor jump. Bear Foot jumped 141.1 feet (43 m)!

World Record Time 4.59

Bear Foot has been around for a long time, but fans still love it! This picture of Bear Foot was taken in 2005.

Monster Trucks of Tomorrow

Today, monster trucks are better liked than ever. They are one of the biggest touring, or traveling, shows in the world. The biggest monster truck racing **series** is the U.S. Hot Rod Association's Monster Jam series. This series puts on drag races and freestyle events across the country. It wows crowds with the coolest monster trucks around.

Fans go wild as the trucks crush cars, spin doughnuts, and race.

As monster-truck owners work to make their trucks cooler and more powerful, these mad machines will go faster and jump higher than ever. Rock on, monster trucks!

Glossary

axles (AK-sulz) Bars on which a wheel or a pair of wheels turns.

championship (CHAM-pee-un-ship) A race held to decide the best, or the winner.

custom (KUS-tum) Made in a certain way for a person.

engines (EN-jinz) Machines inside a car or airplane that make the car or airplane move.

grave (GRAYV) A place where a dead person is laid to rest.

harness (HAR-nes) The ties, bands, and other pieces that hold something or someone in place.

horsepower (HORS-pow-er) The way an engine's power is measured.

mechanics (mih-KA-niks) People who are skilled at fixing machines.

perform (per-FORM) To do something for other people to watch.

predator (PREH-duh-ter) An animal that kills other animals for food.

promoter (pruh-MOH-ter) A person who raises attention about something.

series (SIR-eez) A group of like things that come one after another.

shock absorbers (SHOK ub-SORB-erz) Objects that make the object they are tied to shake less.

spinning doughnuts (SPIN-ing DOH-nuts) Doing a trick in which a driver spins a car around very fast.

wheelies (HWEE-leez) Tricks in which people pull up their front wheels and ride only on their back wheels.

Index

Web Sites

Due to the changing nature of Internet links, PowerKids Press has developed an online list of Web sites related to the subject of this book. This site is updated regularly. Please use this link to access the list: www.powerkidslinks.com/wild/monster/

J
629.224

Poolos, Jamie.

Wild about monster
trucks.

21.25

DATE			